# In the Arms
## of the

# Angels

## True Story of a Daughter's Love
## from the Other Side

Fulton Books
Meadville, PA

Published by Fulton Books 2024

ISBN 979-8-88982-407-7 (paperback)
ISBN 979-8-88982-409-1 (digital)

Printed in the United States of America

DEBRA ANN MACIEL

This book is a dedication to my daughter,
Erica Jean Maciel, my angel who guided me through my
grief with her love, patience, and understanding. She kept me
strong and focused on my path with her loving words.

I t is said that God knew us before we are born. He knows every hair on our head. My story started when my daughter was three years old. I was driving, my mother in the passenger seat, and my daughter Erica at the back in her car seat when we drove passed a house. Erica started to yell out, "Mom, I lived there."

I asked Erica, "What you are talking about?" And she pointed to the house and said that she lived there. I had said to Erica that we never lived there and that she never lived there.

She then said again, "Mom, I lived there. I picked you to be my mother. There were other mothers there, but I picked you."

My mother and I looked at each other in disbelief. We could not believe what Erica was saying. It was never mentioned again, but I always kept it in the back of my mind. The next day, I drove by the house again, and in the front of the house on the lawn was a statue of Mother Mary. I had then known what Erica was trying to tell me. She had remembered being in heaven and seeing Mother Mary when she had picked me for her mother. I had thought what a blessing to hear that my daughter had picked me to be her mother. I had never forgotten this, and each time I remember, I think how wonderful to have heard this from my daughter and to know that we pick our lives.

On Sunday, December 16, 2007, I woke up feeling sad. I sat at the edge of my bed trying to recall if I had a bad dream, but I could not remember. The sadness felt heavy in my chest, and what came to

mind was a pain in my heart not physical pain but emotional pain. I knew something was very wrong, but I did not know what. I did not recall of ever feeling this way, so I did not understand what was going on.

Throughout the day, this feeling stayed with me, and I still could not make sense of it. I started feeling anxious which led to a feeling of something was very wrong. I tried to forget the way I was feeling, for it was a little over a week before Christmas, and I was going to surprise Erica with a real tree this year. I was excited about the thought of surprising her for she always wanted a real tree instead of our artificial one that we had every year. Erica had stayed overnight at her half sister's house to help her with her newborn son.

Erica was excited to be able to spend time with them both. She loved the idea of being an aunt and spending time with her sister. As the day went on, I still could not shake the feeling of anxiety and that something was very wrong. I sat for awhile to think of why I was feeling this way, and it came to me that it could be something about Erica. I had not heard from Erica which she had told me when she left the day before that she would call me that night. Erica would forget when she got busy. She has done it many times, so I really did not think much of it at the time. Then I realized that Erica had not called me today as well. Now my mind is racing along with my heart, and my anxiety is stronger.

All I could think of is something happened to Erica. I tried to push the thought out of my mind, but Erica was going through a battle with drug addiction. She had been on methadone for a week to help her stay away from heroin, the drug she was using. I was proud of her that she made her mind up about staying away from drugs. That she wanted a better life for herself. I have finally felt that I could breathe again and not have to worry if she was going to hurt herself or I was going to get that phone call that every parent dreads when their child is in addiction.

I had tried calling her phone and left several messages but had not heard back from her. I had tried to find her sister's phone number but could not, so all I could do was wait. I was sitting in this anxiety that kept growing stronger and stronger, so I had to keep myself busy.

I started to work on the tree again. I had decided to put the lights on the tree and plugged each one in to make sure that they were working. As I got to the last set of lights that were on the tree, they all went out.

Then the phone rang, and it was Erica's sister. She had told me that Erica had never showed up the night before and was trying to reach her on her phone, but her phone went to messenger, and Erica never returned the phone call. Then she told me that she had received a phone call from someone that she knows, and they told her that Erica was in the hospital.

I had said to her, "What do you mean Erica is in the hospital? What happened to her?"

And her sister replied that was the only information she received. She did not know what had happened to Erica only that she was at the hospital. I had asked for this person's phone number so I could get more information about what was going on with Erica. I had called the number, and a man answered the phone and gave me the same information that was given to Erica's sister that she was in the hospital and that is all that this person knew.

When I hung up the phone, all I could think of is this the reason I was feeling the way that I have been feeling since I woke up? As I was scrambling to look for the number to call the hospital, I called out to God and said, "Please let there be nothing wrong with Erica. Please let it be that she is just hurt, but she is going to be okay." All these thoughts were running in my head, my hands were shaking. My heart felt like it was going to jump out of my chest. My anxiety was unbelievable. I had to sit for a couple of minutes to calm myself down before I made the phone call to the hospital. I just could not function.

Minutes had passed where I could make the phone call and not sound like a frantic mother losing control. The person who answered the phone told me that I had to speak to an officer from the police department, and they gave me the officer's name. I had asked about my daughter, wanted to know if she were okay and what had happened to her and was told by this person on the phone that I needed to call the officer that they could not give me any information.

I kept saying, "This is my daughter. I need to know what is going on. Please tell me what is going on with my daughter. Is she okay? Can I come to the hospital and see her?"

Again, I was told that I needed to call the officer, and I was told they were sorry and hung up. I could not believe this was happening, no information whatsoever. Then I called the police station and ask for the officer and was told that he would call me back. I had to wait fifteen minutes for the officer to call me back, and he would not give me any information as well about my daughter's condition. He went ahead to tell me that he could meet me at the hospital at 6:00 p.m. and he would let me know what is going on.

I had said to him that it would be four hours that I had to wait to find out about my daughter which I felt was not fair to be treated this way. This was my daughter, and I had every right to know what was going on with her, and I should not have to wait for four hours. Still, that did not seem to bother him, and I still had to wait the four hours to find out what was going on with my daughter.

When I hung up the phone, I wanted to scream. I paced the floor as all kinds of thoughts were coming to my mind about what happened to Erica. Why didn't she show up at her sister's? Where did she go? What happened to her? How am I going to be able to wait four hours without any information about her condition? Now the fear of the unknown was on me, and I could not handle everything that I was feeling. I felt as though I was going to explode. I knew that I needed to calm myself down because I needed to let Erica's grandparents know what was going on. They lived downstairs from me, and I did not want them to see me in this condition.

Unfortunately, I exploded and started screaming. I could not take this anymore. My sister who lived upstairs came down after hearing me scream, and I told her what was going on. We both went downstairs to tell Erica's grandparents. My father was close to Erica from the time she was born, and I knew he was going to take it extremely hard. I was afraid of both my parents feeling how I was feeling, so I tried to play it off that it was not as bad as I thought. They knew in the back of their mind just like I did that it did not sound good. All we could do was wait.

I remember when this all started. Erica moved into her first apartment. I was not happy about the location and tried to talk her out of it, but it was her price range, and I had seen how happy she was, so I went along with it. She had purchased all the rooms of furniture, and her grandfather and I fixed her apartment the way that she wanted it to look. We painted every room and put new carpet in the living room and bedrooms. She had a theme for every room. Her windows in the apartment should have been replaced because they did not fit well, so we put plastic on them to keep the cold out.

The property owner said that he was in the process of replacing them but never did. I was not happy about this, but Erica did not want me to say anything to the property owner. I was happy for her. I'd seen the happiness in her face as everything was coming together for her. I was still nervous about her living alone in that location, especially with her windows, the way that they were, so I visited her when she did not have friends over. I knew that she was happy having her own place, and it also helped our relationship. We seem to get along better and enjoyed each other's company. I was immensely proud of her having an excellent job and being responsible with her life. It had put my mind at ease that I did not have to worry about her as much. She was finally living her life on her terms.

Erica had been in her apartment for about six months when her apartment was broken into. They climbed through her window and walked out the front door with her brand-new TV and other personal items. I felt so horrible that she had to go through this—someone going through your house, invading your privacy and taking items that belonged to you. I had seen the disappointment in her face, and she was also afraid knowing that someone was in her house and not knowing if they were going to come back. I also found out that this was not the first time that there were two other times that her house was broken into.

Now I was fearing for her safety. I did not like the idea that she was there alone. She had told me that she was having friends sleeping over because she was afraid to be alone. This went on for a few months, and I had seen a substantial change in Erica because of what happened. She was depressed, so I tried to visit her as much as I

could, and I also suggested that she come over and spend time at the house with me. I was upset with the property owner as well, about replacing the windows.

If the windows were replaced and locked, no one could have climbed through them. I had finally convinced Erica to give up her apartment, put her furniture in storage, and move back home with me. I had told her that I would help her find another apartment in a better location, and she agreed. I had helped her pack everything up, but I knew that this was a great disappointment for her. I felt so terrible. She had worked hard to have the apartment the way she wanted it with time and money, and now she had to give it up.

When Erica moved back home, she grew increasingly depressed. I tried to speak with her, but she kept growing distant from me. We would argue, and then we both get upset with each other. I did not know what to do for her, so I let her be so we would not be arguing all the time. She was seeing someone for a while. He had a job that would keep him away for months at a time, but he would call her all the time on the phone.

When he was home, Erica would stay over at his place. Erica seemed happy for a while. She was happy when he was home, and she got to spend time with him. They seem to do a lot together, taking day trips and some overnights. I was happy for her because I had seen a change in her that she was happy again. Our relationship started getting better again. She would call me more often and talk about the places that she went with him and how happy she was. I had thought that he was good for Erica and that he loved her and cared for her, and hopefully, someday this would turn into something more.

They were seeing each other for a couple of years when I started seeing a change in Erica. When he would go away for work, Erica would come back home, and she would close herself in her room. Many times, I heard her arguing with him on the phone which led to her crying through the night. I tried to talk to her about it, but she just shut me out. My heart was breaking for her. I wanted her to be happy. This went on every time he was away at work, and Erica would be crying on the phone and locked in her bedroom.

Some of the conversations I could hear and did not like. He was trying to change my daughter into someone that he wanted and not who she was. I could not understand why he would want to change Erica. She was a loving person who would do anything for anyone. She was kindhearted, intelligent, and beautiful. I know that he was verbally abusing her over the phone which I tried to talk to her about and told her that she should not be taking that from him and that if it was going to continue, she should look to breaking it off with him.

When he was home from work, I had found out that he was not only verbally abusing her but also physically abusing her. Many times, in the middle of the night, he would call my house and tell me to get my daughter, or he was going to call the police on her. I had argued with him many times about him keeping his hands off her and that he had no right touching her. This went on for several months, and Erica took it because she loved him. I was glad when he was not around because he was not physically hurting her, but he was mentally hurting her.

I tried many times to talk to her about her relationship with him. I spoke about it that it was not love but abuse, and he had no right treating her that way. I knew that Erica had a low self-esteem, but I could not understand why. She was smart, she had an excellent job, she was caring and loving, so I could not understand why she would allow him to treat her that way. All I could think of is that he kept telling her that she was not up to his expectations because I know that he wanted to change her. As far as I was concern, he did not deserve her.

One day, when he was away at work, Erica decided to go for a ride with a friend on his motorcycle. At a green light, her friend popped the front of the bike up, and Erica fell off the back. Erica was taken to the hospital, and she found out that she damaged her coccyx bone, which is the tailbone. They sent her home with a prescription of Percocet 30s for the pain. I had told Erica that they were addicting and that to make sure that she only took what the prescription said for her to take.

She had made an appointment with an orthopedic, and he informed her that she would need surgery. In the meantime, he was

supplying her with Percocets because of the level of pain that she was having. I had asked her when she was going to have surgery, but she kept saying that she was not going to do the surgery yet. This went on for several months, and I found out that she was hopping from doctor to doctor and getting prescription after prescription of Percocets.

I was upset over what she was doing. She was taking more than what was prescribed. I told her that I was going to contact the doctor and tell him what was going on. She was having problems with feeling her legs, they would go numb. I had told her that she needed to go for the surgery because things were getting worse for her. She was not working, and she was hooked on the Percocets. I could not believe a doctor would keep giving her a prescription of an addicting substance instead of telling her no more before she got addicted and that she needed to do the surgery. Well, the doctor stopped the prescriptions and left her to figure out how to get out of her addiction, and her boyfriend had the solution—heroin.

Now Erica was a heroin addict, and so the nightmare began. I had found out a few weeks earlier from Erica's sister that Erica's boyfriend was using heroin. I had mentioned that to Erica which she denied. I did not know where to start to help her, but I knew I needed to do something. I figured the best way to start would be to go through her bedroom which I did. I found needles in the closet, under the bed, in between the mattress, and in between her clothes that were thrown all over the room. I felt so overwhelmed as a parent because I did not know what to do at this point. I had tried talking to her, but she kept shutting me out. She just did not want to hear what I had to say.

I tried to reason with her to help her that did not work. She would stay away for months at a time so I would not know what was going on with her. She would call from time to time, but I could tell from her words slurring that she was high. At this point, I was very depressed. Each night I would cry myself to sleep because I did not know what to do for her. There were times when I would run into her, and she must have seen the shock on my face and unfortunately the disappointment.

She was very skinny, pale-looking, and had a lot of acne on her face. I kept wondering why she would do this to herself. I wanted to hug her and bring her home and tell her everything was going to be okay, but I did not know how to fix the situation she was in. I was afraid that Erica was going to die. It was on my mind every minute of the day and especially at night. I felt pain in my heart to know that she was ruining her life and her body and that she did not seem to care.

As a parent, you have hopes and dreams for your child. You want them to be happy and successful in whatever they decide to do with their life. If they choose to be with someone, you hope that, that someone cares and loves them not mentally and physically abuse them. The dreams I had for my daughter had turned into a nightmare. I did not know how to help her. I knew nothing about addiction, how it controls the mind, changes the personality, and causes cravings so severe for the drug. It will bring you to places and actions that you would have never thought possible of yourself.

This is all to obtain money or the drug itself, so you do not go into withdrawals. I wanted to give that doctor a piece of my mind. How many others had he consciously wrote a prescription for where they got addicted? How could he have not known? I should have done something about it before it got out of hand. The doctor should have lost his license for writing that many prescriptions for Percocets and then leaving my daughter to fend for herself. I was so angry at myself for trusting this doctor.

This spiraling lifestyle went on for more than two years. Often, I would see Erica and try to talk to her about getting help, but I could not get through to her. I had heard from some of her friends that they had seen her and that she looked terrible. All I kept thinking about was she is going to overdose, and I was going to lose my daughter. I would dread when the phone rang. I would always have this sinking feeling inside of me each night and wake with the same pain from the night before. I would go to work and try to block my mind from thinking about Erica so I would be able to do my job. Easier said than done. This made me feel guilty.

I am her mother, and I should be able to do something to help her, but what? I did not understand what she was going through. I had thought that if she wanted to stop using drugs she could, she just did not want to, and with this in mind I was angry with her. I did not know of anyone who was going through this with their child. I felt alone in this with no solutions. Erica's grandfather many times tried to speak to her about going for help, and of course, she kept promising him that she would. You could see the disappointment on his face and the fear in his eyes as he spoke to her. He knew as well as I did that this was not good, and at any time, we could lose her.

Addiction controls the part of the brain that controls your emotions—the pleasure part of the brain where you feel happy and excited. Using heroin, it starts damaging the cells in that part of the brain which causes the brain to be numb in that area. You do not feel. You do not care. I did not know this at the time. Erica was feeling pain physically and mentally before she started using.

When the drug starts wearing off which is called withdrawals that pain starts coming back physically at first. Your whole body hurts so bad that you take more of the drug, so you do not feel the pain. The withdrawals also cause cravings for the drug. It makes you think that you are going to die if you do not put the drug back into your body. It is a vicious cycle of thinking how you are going to get money to get the drug, so you are not sick. I knew that she had money in the bank which she was using to pay for the heroin. All I could think of was that she was going to die. I thought about this every minute of the day and night that it consumed me with fear and caused me to be depressed.

I had learned from someone that I could go to court and have my daughter sectioned so she could get help. I was informed by the court that there was a section at a women's prison where she could get the help she needs. She could detox there, and they would help her through it. I was not happy about sending my daughter to a prison. I had heard stories about what does happen there, fighting and having to watch your back for all kinds of reasons.

I did not know what else to do. I thought if there is a section that helps with drug addiction, then at least she would be clean, and she will not die. I was afraid for her, but I was more afraid of her losing her life. Erica was there for about four months, and I learned that she did not receive the care that she needed to detox. She had to go through the pain of detoxing without comfort medication. Post-acute withdrawal is a painful process. It is severe pain throughout your body which lasts for many weeks. I was terribly upset to learn of the pain she had to go through, but I also thought that she will learn from this and stay away from drugs. Going through the withdrawal and being in the environment that she was in would be enough to want to stay clean. It was a hard lesson, and I prayed that she would not want to go through it again.

Erica had called me at least twice a week. When she started feeling better, she told me that she was no longer going to use heroin. She said she wanted to move on with her life. She wanted to go back to college and become a nurse. She had been a certified nursing assistant and had studied to be a medication technician before her life got upside down. I was so happy to hear this and felt that I had made the right decision to have her committed. I was finally getting my daughter back, and that was the happiest feeling in the world. I told her that I would help her and when she got back on her feet, I would help her find an apartment.

She seemed excited and happy to know that I was going to stand by her and help her anyway I could. I told her that she could come back home and slowly put her life back together. Each time she called I encouraged her and told her that I was happy that she was moving on with her life. I had told her that each day her life would get better and that I would be there for her. I explained to her that I did not know what else to do for her when she was using heroin and that I was afraid that I was going to lose her. I told her that I loved her and wanted the best for her. She said she was sorry and understood why I did what I had to do.

For the first time in a long time, I was finally feeling hopeful. When Erica returned home, she had signed up for a group on substance abuse. The group met once a week, and I drove her and picked her up. I tried to encourage her to see a therapist because she was suffering from depression and PTSD. I explained to her that if she

talked about her problems to a therapist, it would relieve some of her pain. Erica was not interested in speaking with a therapist, so I did not press the issue.

Now when I look back, I wished I had. Things would have been different. It did not take long before Erica was in touch with her boyfriend again. I had wished she would have moved on from him. I was sure that he was still using, and I did not want Erica to start up again. She had told me that he was not using anymore, but I knew that she was not telling me the truth.

I had decided to change my phone number and asked Erica not to give it out. I did not want her to get involved with the people that she had done drugs with, but before long, they were calling again. I was upset with her because I felt that she did not understand that these people were not her friends. I had noticed that she was becoming depressed and confining herself to her room when I came home from work. She then started leaving the house in the middle of the night, and I knew that it was only a matter of time before she started using again.

I tried many times to speak to her about going back to college for nursing. I even told her that if she did not want to work that she could just concentrate on school. She had stopped going to group, and then I knew that the nightmare of her using again was back. I had to know for sure so when she had left the house I decided to go through her room. I hoped that I would not find anything, but unfortunately, I found needles again.

My heart fell to my feet. I thought how she could put herself through this again. Why didn't she go to therapy for her depression? I did not know what to do. Should I section her again? I tried to talk to her many times, but she just sat there nodding out, and her eyes rolling back in her head. I could not take it anymore seeing her this way. I felt ashamed of her and felt ashamed of myself for feeling this way. I could not take looking at her anymore, so I told her that she had a choice to get help or she would have to leave. She chose to leave.

The situation was hopeless. Before she left, I told her that if she decided to change her mind and get help, I would be there for her. All she had to do was call. She told me that it was too hard to stop, and she left. Every day it took all my strength to get out of bed. I wanted to pull the covers over my head and wait till everything changed for the better, but I had to go to work and face this reality. From time to time, I would run into Erica, and she looked worse than the last time I had seen her. She was so skinny. I knew she was not eating. Her hair was unkept, and her clothes were not clean. It broke my heart each time I had seen her this way, but I acted as if I did not notice the condition she was in. I remembered how she was always conscious about how she looked. She had beautiful thick curly hair, always wore makeup, and liked to wear nice clothes. She was now a different person standing in front of me whom I did not know. My heart cried. I wanted my Erica back.

Months had gone by when I had received a phone call from Erica. The call was from the house of correction, and Erica was on the other end of the phone. She had been arrested for using. I was sorry for her being in that place, but at the same time, I felt relieved. She was no longer going to be able to use, and this might wake her up to what she was doing to herself. I thought, *Here we go again*, but I felt a glimmer of hope again. I had taken her phone calls each time she called.

I knew each time she called that she was starting to feel better because she would talk about how she was not going to use anymore and that she wanted her life back. I had hopes again for her and myself. I tried to encourage her each time she called about the things she had wanted to do in her life and that she could still do. I knew she so wanted this for herself, and I was happy to hear her plans. I was looking forward to having her back home. She was going to be released two weeks before Christmas. I had missed my daughter and could not wait to see her.

I kept hoping that this time she is going to stay away from the drugs. How could she keep doing this to herself? I know she wanted a better life for herself. She still had the hopes and dreams for her life, and I could not understand why she could not move forward with them. I knew she had depression and PTSD, and she needed to take care of it through counseling. I had to convince her somehow to see a therapist and go on medication to take care of her depression. She

needed to know that her dreams are still possible and that she needed to concentrate on that. I had told her that I would help her because I wanted her to be happy and achieve what she wants for her life. I was her mother, and I loved her and would do anything for her to be happy.

The day came for her release, and I was there to pick her up. When she came out, she looked happy. She had gained weight. Erica told me that she was going to use methadone to help her stay away from heroin and that there was a clinic near to our home. She made an appointment the next day, and each morning before I went to work, I would take her to the clinic for her treatment and then take her home. These first couple of days, I had seen a change in her, and I was starting to feel hopeful again. I did not want to pressure her right away about going back to school. I wanted her to be able to breathe again and enjoy Christmas. After the holidays, we would talk about seeing a therapist and going on medication for her depression.

On Saturday of the first week of going to the clinic, Erica told me that because we were going to have a snowstorm over the weekend, the clinic gave her Sunday and Monday's doses to take home. I had thought that it was strange that she just started on the methadone, and they were already giving her doses to take home on her own. She assured me that she knew how much to take and that she would be okay. I took her home, and I went to work feeling uneasy about it.

Upon returning home from work, I had pulled into the driveway to see a woman going through my daughter's car. The woman was startled to see me, and I asked her what she was doing and who she was. She replied that she was helping Erica find out what was wrong with her car. I told her that I did not believe her for she had all the doors open as well as the trunk. I told her to get the hell out of here, and she walked down the driveway and into a car that had people inside. I locked her car and went upstairs to find out what was going on.

I found my daughter filling up a bag with clothes. I asked her about the woman outside going through her car. Erica had no idea that she was in her car. As I was speaking with her, the driver was lying on the horn. I asked Erica what was going on, and who were these people. She told me that they were going to give her a ride to her sister's house that was why she was packing a bag. She was going to help her sister with the baby and was sleeping there overnight.

I did not trust these people and told my daughter to call me later so I know she was all right. She said, "I love you, Mom, and I will call you later." I felt uneasy about these people, but I had to trust her judgment. Erica had always seen the good in people. I did not think after seeing her going through my daughter's car that they were anything but trouble. I was uneasy all night about Erica being with them. Also for the fact that this woman was older than me, and why was she hanging around with my daughter.

Erica had not driven her car for several months because I had taken the ignition key off her key ring and replaced it with the valet key. She was driving high, and I was afraid that she would hurt someone or herself. She thought that there was something wrong with the ignition, so I let her think it. She had no money to fix the car, so it sat in the yard for months. I thought once she showed that she was moving on with her life and staying away from drugs she would have the car back. But until then, I had to let her believe that there was something wrong with the ignition.

I had never received a phone call from Erica, but she would forget sometimes so that was what I had thought. I was happy that she was going to spend time with her sister and the baby, but I was still uneasy about these people. Especially a woman who looked to be in her late-fifties and hanging around with a twenty-seven-year-old. I had wished that I had taken her instead of her getting into the car with them. This was something that I would regret for the rest of my life.

The following morning Sunday, December 16, 2007, a day I will never forget, I was waiting for 6:00 p.m. to meet the officer at the hospital to find out what was going on with my daughter. I kept pushing the thoughts of her being hurt or worst out of my head. I needed to distract myself, so I decided to work on the Christmas tree again. Erica was going to be surprised with the tree. I had picked up the tree the following night after she left, so she did not see it. She

liked real trees, and I wanted her to be happy because of everything she had gone through the past years. Then I started to remember how I felt when I woke in the morning, the anxiety, and the feeling of loss in my heart.

Was this a sign of the pain that was to come? I did not want to think of this. I kept telling myself that she was going to be okay, nothing is wrong. I could not take this anxiety any longer and cried out to God to give me a sign that Erica was okay. Then my heart sank, and I realized that the reason I was going to the hospital was to identify my daughter. Please God, this cannot be happening. How am I going to live without my daughter? My heart felt as if someone had put their hand in my chest and was squeezing my heart. The pain was unbearable. I wanted to die. I would not be able to live without my daughter.

My thoughts kept playing over and over in my head of what had happened to her, and I did not want to think anymore of the way I was thinking. I knew she never made it to her sister's house, so she had to have been with the people who picked her up the night before—the woman who had been going through her car. What had they done to her? I felt as though I was in and out of reality. I had also believed that I was in shock. I thought that if I go and lie down, I will fall asleep and wake up everything will be okay and that this was not real, but it was a living nightmare, and I wanted it to stop.

I wanted Erica to walk through the door and say, "I am home, Mom," but I knew that was not going to happen. I was never going to see her alive again, never going to hear her voice, and never going to be able to tell her that I love her. My heart was so filled with pain. My mind was spinning out of control. What had happened to her? How did she die? Did she suffer? She had her whole life ahead of her. She was only twenty-seven years old with hopes and dreams for her life. She was on methadone. She was gone.

I sat on the floor in front of the Christmas tree and just cried. I was putting up the tree to surprise Erica, and now she will never see it. I started to feel angry. This was not fair to Erica or myself. I started pulling the lights off the tree in a fit of anger. I thought, *This is it. The tree is not going up.* I dragged the tree through the house down the stairs and in the backyard. I did not want to look at the tree. I put the decorations away and then sat in disbelief and cried. My world was ending, and there was nothing that I could do about it.

It was now 5:30. Time to go to the hospital to identify Erica's body. On the way there, I thought that this is it. This was final, no getting a chance to hope that the outcome could be different. This was hard to comprehend, but I knew that I had to face what was coming. I could not hope anymore that they made a mistake and that it was not her. When I had arrived at the hospital, I was taken to a family room where the officer whom I spoke with on the phone was waiting. He informed me that Erica was deceased and that she was a Jane Doe and that I needed to identify her.

I asked what had happen to my daughter and was told by the officer that she had died from an overdose. She died at the woman's house who was going through her car the night before. I told the officer that she had been clean and was using methadone, so how could this happen? Why didn't someone help her? He had no answers for me and no compassion.

I was totally discussed with his lack of information and his attitude. I had asked if he was going to have answers for me, and he expressed no concern. I had told him I wanted to see my daughter, and he said that they were getting her ready for me to identify her. Unbelievable that I still had to wait to see my daughter. I could not stand looking at the officer while I was waiting. I had wished he would leave the room. I had so much anger in me because of his lack of compassion, and I also knew that he was not going to investigate my daughter's death, and that made me sick to my stomach as well as angry.

A half hour had passed, and a hospital worker entered the room and told me that I could see my daughter. We took an elevator to the ground floor and walked down the hall. I had noticed a room on the right-hand side of the hall, and as we got closer, I'd seen my daughter's curly hair. My heart sank to my feet. There was my daughter lying in a body bag. There was no hope anymore. I had noticed that she had dried blood coming from her ear and her mouth. I had asked about the blood, and I was told that it happens in these circumstances.

I asked the officer again about investigating her death, and I was told that there was going to be an autopsy done on her. I had told the officer that if she died from an overdose, why then would it be necessary for an autopsy? His reply was it was going to be done, and I had no say in it. I had asked if he was going to investigate, and his reply was that Erica had brought the drugs there and that her purse was filled with drug paraphernalia. I asked the officer if the other people were using, and he said that he did not believe so. I did not believe him. What kind of people do not call for help when someone is overdosing? I would get answers from her autopsy. I did not want to think about what they were going to do to her body, but I needed answers.

I was not told when the medical examiner was going to release my daughter's body, so I went to the funeral home the next day to plan arrangements. Here I was picking out a casket for my daughter.

Nothing seemed real. I felt as though I was in a dark hole, and I could not find my way out. I did not know how I was going to get through this. The pain was so unbearable, and that was the only thing that I could feel. I cried day and night. I wondered each day about what had happened to her. Why didn't they help her, and why was the police taking their word for what had happened, instead of doing an investigation?

I walked the floors in my home for days. My parents talked me into putting up the Christmas tree for Erica. I thought that she would still see the tree and would be happy. It was three days when my daughter's body was released to the funeral home. The funeral home had called me and told me that my daughter would be ready on Friday for her wake, and her funeral would be the following day.

I thought to myself, *How I was going to get through this?* I would look at my daughter's room and know that she would never be here again. She would not be sleeping in her bed anymore. She would not be wearing her clothes anymore, and I would not see her here anymore. It was too hard to bear. I asked God for strength to please help me get through this. Nothing seemed real. It was like being outside yourself and watching what was going on. I kept asking myself, how is this happening? It felt like time had stood still. I could not go back, and I could not move forward. I was stuck in this moment in time.

I was starting to feel like a failure as a mother. I should have drove her myself to her sister's. I knew that these people were up to no good. I was not there to protect her. She was alone and defenseless. She was still fighting her addiction. I should have been more supportive. I should have showed her and said to her more times that I loved her and was proud of her. She is my daughter, the most important person in my life, and I hoped that she knew.

I should have, I should have, I should have. This is what I was drowning in day after day. I was causing myself to be deeper and deeper in a hole which was so deep. There was no way out. I kept telling myself to snap out of it that Erica's wake and funeral was coming up, and I had to be strong, but the pain in me was so overwhelming. My mind kept going back to the night that she left. I needed answers to what had happened to her. I knew that she had died from an overdose, but why? It made me sick inside to know that she was alone with these people, and no one helped her. Erica was a loving person who would do anything for anyone.

The day came of her wake. I made the calling hours 5:00 p.m. to 9:00 p.m. I along with my family could arrive an hour earlier before anyone else arrived. I was shaking all day till the time I arrived. I did not want to see her that way, but I had missed seeing her. When I walked into the funeral home and seen my daughter lying there in a casket, my heart dropped to my feet. It took all the strength in my body to walk over to her. I wanted to run in the opposite direction and pretend this was not happening. But it was happening, and I had to find the strength to get through the next hours and greet everyone who came to pay their respects. My beautiful Erica, whom I had seen days ago walking out the door, telling me that she loved me and will call me later, was now lying here, and I will never hear her speak to me again. I wanted to scream. How am I going to live without Erica? Why did this have to happen?

I went through the motions of greeting and thanking people for coming. I kept watching the door to make sure these people did not come in. I would have had them thrown out. I felt as though I

was going to collapse each time I stood. I felt that the pain inside me was taking all the strength that I had left. I was sick to my stomach and wanted to lie down and die myself. I kept looking over at Erica, hoping that now she is at peace and that she does not have to suffer her addiction anymore or her problems that she was having.

I was hoping that she was happy and was with Jesus on the other side. I felt some comfort in this. I knew Erica believed that Jesus was her Lord and Savior and that she was home with him. I knew that this was going to be the last time I would be able to see her, so I was close to her many times as I could. I held her hand and stroked her head and told her that I loved her and was going to miss her. I told her that I was sorry that this had happened, and I was sorry that I could not be with her.

As I was speaking to her, I had noticed that her mouth was crooked. I had called over the person who was working at the funeral home, and she said that it was because of the autopsy and that they did not put her mouth back together correctly. This made me furious to know that they left her this way that they did not have the decency to fix her mouth. As I was looking at her, I heard my daughter's voice in my head say, "Oh wow, I look like crap."

I stood there in disbelief. What did I just hear? Am I losing it? I looked around to see if someone had said something, but there was no one around me. I realized that it was Erica's voice, but I thought that I was going crazy. It must be the grief. It was so overwhelming that it was making me hear things. I did not tell anyone in fear of people thinking that I was going crazy. That is what I thought so would everyone else.

Many people attended her wake. Erica was a kindhearted beautiful person. She seen the good in people which at times made her vulnerable to people who had bad intentions. I had the feeling, call it mother's intuition, but I felt my daughter had been intentionally overdosed. When I went home that night, my home had never felt so empty. I kept playing in my head the last time I had seen Erica alive. I felt alone, and the pain was hard to bear. Then I thought about what I had heard, Erica's voice speaking to me. I thought would it not be great if I did hear her. It sounded just like her.

I had decided to call my friend and tell her about what I had heard. She would understand because she has a gift. I had known Chris for many years, and she would not think that I was losing it. She had told me that she knew someone who was friends with a medium and would see if she could get me an appointment. I had never gone to a medium, but I was open to it, for I wanted to know if I really heard my daughter, and I wanted to speak to Erica. I wanted her to know that I love her and was proud of her.

The next day was Erica's funeral. I arrived at the funeral home knowing that this was going to be the last time that I was going to see her. Everyone was asked to go to their vehicles as I watched the funeral director arrange pictures, notes, and flowers in her casket. I stood there watching as she closed her casket, and a feeling of dread washed over me. I knew I was never going to see my daughter's face again. My heart was in so much pain. We headed to the church. It was full, and there were people standing. I was happy to know that these people cared about my daughter and me as well.

I cried through the whole service to the point that my head was shaking so much that I could not lift my head. I was so weak from crying. I could hardly stand or walk. We then arrived at the cemetery. I did not want to leave her there alone. I wanted to stay until she was buried, but I was told by friends that it would be worst to see her put in the ground. As we drove away, I was looking at her casket and thinking why this had to happen.

That night, I had decided that I could not live without Erica. The pain was too much for me to bear. I had a bottle of sleeping pills and a glass of water on my nightstand. I thought it was going to be easy, just go to sleep and wake up on the other side where I would be with Erica. I was sitting on the edge of my bed and looking at the bottle when it hit me. If I take my life, I will not be with Erica because this was wrong to take your life that God has given you.

When you take your life, you end up in a different place, and Erica would not be there. What would be the point? I wanted to be with Erica, now I am going to have to live with the pain of my daughter not being here. I did not know how I was going to do this,

but I had no choice. I had thought about my family, and I did not want to put them through any more pain as well.

I asked God every day to give me strength. The idea of not seeing my daughter for the rest of my life was so unbearable and weakening that I did not know how I was going to move on. I felt stuck in this grief. The pain in my heart was so strong. It caused me to have panic attacks. I walked around my house every day from room to room. I did not know how to handle this pain. I went to the cemetery every day and cried at her grave.

Strangers stopped to help me. They tried to comfort me, but I wanted to be alone. I wanted to be with my daughter. I did not want to be here anymore. I asked God what I did wrong to have to lose my daughter. I thought that it was my fault that my daughter was gone because of the choices that I had made in my life. Erica had to suffer because of me. I had wished that God had took me instead. Parents are not supposed to bury their children. She was my only child, and now I was alone in this pain. All the dreams that I had hoped for Erica was buried with her.

Each day I kept thinking about how Erica had died. I wondered if she knew she was going to die. Did she feel pain? Did she suffer? Did these people hurt her? I needed answers, so I decided to call the detective that was at the hospital. I had asked why these people did not help my daughter. The response was that my daughter took the drug, went and lie down, and the people went to bed. I had told them that my daughter was going to her sister's house that this did not sound right. I was told that the case was closed and no investigation.

The police took the word of the people as to what happened, and the case was closed within a twenty-four-hour period. I could not believe how incompetent this sounded. What if it were their child, I do not think it would have not been investigated. I know the police thought she was just another addict and she brought it on herself. I could tell by his attitude and lack of compassion. You never think that this situation will ever happen to you. You do not realize when you hear about other people who had lost their child, the unbelievable pain that they are going through, until you go through it yourself.

It changes you and the pain never goes away. You learn to live with the pain because you do not have a choice. You do not want to remember your child with pain, but it is hard not to. You want to remember the happy times that you spent with them, but the pain is there. You look around at your family and friends, and you see that life goes on, but you wonder how you are going to get back in life. It is like your stuck in sorrow and pain, and you cannot see yourself moving forward.

You feel like crawling in a corner and hoping no one will see you. You wake up in the morning, and for a few seconds, there is nothing in your mind, and then it hits you like a ton of bricks. The pain is back, and you know why. I called them reality checks. The day starts and ends the same way with pain and sorrow and missing my daughter. I did not know how to move forward from this because I felt consumed in this pain.

Erica was buried on Saturday, and Christmas was the following Tuesday. I did not want anything to do with Christmas. My family still exchanged gifts and tried to get me involved. I sat there numb to what was going on around me. I looked at them and thought, *How could they still celebrate?* Erica was just buried, and she had always celebrated with us, and now she is not here. My heart is broken. Why would they think that I could still celebrate? I know that they meant well to try to push me to move forward, but it was too soon. I was angry and told them so. Life does not move on for me. My daughter is gone. How could they be so insensitive?

One night as I lie in bed, I heard a noise that was a sound of tapping on glass. It was coming from the light on my nightstand which was on the side of my bed. I got up to look to see if anything was hitting the light, and nothing was. The noise continued, but I had no idea where it was coming from, so I did not bother myself with it. This noise that sounded like tapping had happened many times while I was in bed. Then it started in the kitchen when I would sit at my table, and the tapping would come from over the table where there was a ceiling fan with lights. I could not figure out what

was going on. This had continued for several days—the light on the nightstand and the lights over the kitchen table. I did not know what to make of it.

At this time, I had one more week of paid time off from work. I was using my vacation time, and I could not see myself going back. I did not know how I was going to be able to function at work. I knew that it was not good for me to stay home and cry all day. It was making me sick. I knew I had to learn how to function or to find normalcy whatever that was. Being home all day and my daughter not here anymore was draining the life out of me. I felt weak from crying all day, and I did not want to eat. I just wanted my daughter back. I wanted this nightmare to be over. Nothing seemed real anymore. I talked to my friend Chris and asked her to reach out to her friend who knew the medium. I thought it would be easier for me to go back to work if I had heard from Erica. I knew that she was happy because she was on the other side with our Lord, and she would be with my grandparents. They would take care of her. I just wanted to speak to her and tell her that I love her and I miss her.

Chris had reached out to her friend to make an appointment for me to speak with the medium. The medium had said that for two weeks a spirit was speaking to her named Erica. She did not know who Erica was. Erica had told the medium that she needs to contact her mother. Of course, this woman had no idea of who I was until she was told that I would like to speak to her. She had asked her friend to ask Chris what my daughter's name was, and when she was told that it was Erica, she had asked for my phone number and said she would call me the following night.

When my friend Chris told me this, I could not believe what I was hearing. Erica was trying to contact this woman to speak to me. I felt so happy at that moment and looked forward to speaking with my daughter the next night. I was anxious all day waiting to talk to my daughter. It made me feel so happy to know that my daughter was trying to reach out to me through this woman. She did not want it to end with her not being here. She wanted to speak to me. I thought I will find out exactly what had happened to her. The anticipation was exciting and yet painful.

The medium called around 6:00 p.m., and the first message was that I was not going crazy. Erica had reached out to this woman every day for the past two weeks saying that she had to contact her mother. Erica had told this woman that I can hear her and that I heard her at her wake. She had said what I had heard her say which was that she looked terrible. Erica had tried to speak to me several times during the two weeks but because of me crying all the time, I could not hear her.

Erica explained that she was tapping on the glass to get my attention so she could speak to me, but I did not hear her voice. I was so happy to hear that she was happy. She had said that she was with her great grandparents and with her father. That it was beautiful there where she felt no pain or sorrow but just love. My heart felt full of peace at this time, and we spoke for an hour. She told me she was sorry that this had happened, and she felt no pain. She said she closed her eyes, but before she drifted off, she said a prayer which was, "Now I lay me down to sleep, I pray the Lord my soul to keep. If I should die before I wake, I pray the Lord my soul to take."

She also said as she was taken over to the other side, she asked, "What was going to happen to my mother? Was she going to be okay?" Her guide told her that I would be okay. Erica told me that she was always going to be around me and helping me to get through this. What a wonderful gift that I have to be able to communicate with my daughter and to know that she was happy and with family on the other side. I thank God for this precious gift.

During our talk, Erica's cat, Tang, had jumped onto the table and broke off a piece of eucalyptus from the vase of flowers. The cat started chewing the flower, so I took it off her so she would not get sick. I took the piece of eucalyptus and smelled it, and I heard the medium on the phone say, "Whoa." I asked her what was wrong, and she told me that Erica had just put the smell of eucalyptus to her nose. I could not believe what she was telling me. I had told her that I just had smelled a piece of the flower. We both had goose bumps. That was my confirmation from my daughter that she was near me, and what I was being told was true.

Erica spoke about how beautiful it was there. How vibrant the colors were that was not the same on earth. She spoke about always feeling love that it was all around her. I did not want to hang up with the medium, but I thanked her for helping me communicate with Erica. She spoke with me for an hour, and I will never forget what she had done for me. She brought me a sense of peace. When we hung up, I heard my daughter speaking to me. She had told me that she loved me and missed me. She said she was sorry that she would not be here anymore but was here in spirit. She had told me that she will always be around me and will be there to help me get through the loss of her not being here. I felt comfort in knowing that it was important for my daughter to do this for me. I know that she loves me and wants to comfort me in my grief. I know she was sorry for having me go through this. I will always be grateful to her for wanting to do this for me. That night was the first night that I had sleep peacefully without crying myself to sleep. I knew Erica was safe and happy.

The following day, I had tried to hold on to the feeling of peace knowing Erica was around me and that she was happy. She had told me that she had meet Jesus and she had felt his love for her. I thought about this all the time, but the reality was that she was no longer here, and so the pain was back in my life. If only we can hang on to the fact that we do not die if we believe in God and Jesus and that our loved ones are always around to help us. But the reality for me was that she was not here physically for me to see and be a part of my life, so the grief took over.

Every day since the phone call from the medium, I was able to hear my daughter speak to me. I felt so blessed to be able to hear and speak to my daughter, but it did not seem like reality to me. This was something new to me that I never experienced before, and it did not seem real. It was like living in two different worlds at the same time. The only people that I had talked about this experience with was my friend Chris and my parents.

My friend Chris believed me and spoke to me every night for years to help me with my grief. I could not have had a better person in my life to help me get through this. I will always be grateful to her for her love and compassion in helping me through this. My parents believed me because Erica let them know that she was around. A vase in my parent's bathroom went flying across the room when my mother was in the room. The vase broke, and Erica told me to tell my mother that she was sorry that she had hit the vase too hard. She said she had just wanted it to move so my mother would know that she was there, but she sent it across the room by accident.

Well, if they had any doubt, they do not now. It was wonderful to be able to talk to my daughter every day. She would tell me how she was going to be there for me to help me through this and that she loved me. She would tap on lights to get my attention so I would know that she was there. Many times, I would talk to my friend Chris on the phone, and Erica would tell me to tell her hello. At times it did not seem real to me that I could communicate with my daughter. It was a blessing from God. I do not know how my life would have turned out if I could not hear my daughter.

Erica kept telling me to journal which would help me with my pain. I did not listen to her. I wished I had listened to her about keeping a journal. My anxiety led to panic attacks, which my doctor prescribed medication. I did not know how to handle this pain, but I knew that I did not want it to control my life. Everyone was going on with their life, but I did not know how to go on. I felt as though I was standing still, and life was moving around me. I did not want to be involved with life anymore, but I knew I had no choice. All I could think about was I was never going to see my daughter again. I will not be able to see her get married, have children, or be a nurse which she had wanted as a career. I could not see myself moving forward without my daughter. I felt as though I died along with her, and there was no coming back.

I had returned to work after weeks of being home from the time my daughter passed. I did not want to go back. I wanted to stay home and speak with my daughter, but I needed to return for my mental health, and of course I had bills to pay. I was afraid of going deeper into depression and not finding my way out. I know that some people would think why I would be depressed if I could

hear my daughter, but my reality was that she still was not living here anymore.

I could not see her or touch her, and that is what made me depressed. My first day back to work, I felt different inside like I was not myself anymore. I did not know what to expect if I could even do my job. I know the pain in my heart showed in my eyes for I seen the pity in people's faces who I worked with. They meant well, but it was hard to see it. I just wanted to be myself again no pain. I wanted to be normal, but was this my new normal? I was deep inside my grief, and it was hard to function at work. I went through the motions during work and could not wait to get back home.

Many times, I wanted to give up and run out the door. I felt my daughter was there waiting for me at home. There were times when the pain was so overwhelming in work that I would go to the restroom to cry. It was hard to keep my composure because the pain in my heart was constant even when I was trying to keep my mind busy with work. I wanted the pain to go away. I did not want to remember my daughter with pain. I wanted to remember her with good memories of love and happiness.

When I returned home every day from work, I had my dog, Dakota, to help me through my grief. He was wonderful. He was a yellow lab full of energy. I would pick him up after work from the doggy day care center, and he would keep my mind busy with playing and walking. The weeks that I was home from work, I would have never had gotten out of bed if it were not for him being with me. He was a wonderful blessing in my life. At night when we settled down, it is when the pain was stronger. This is when my friend Chris was there for me. She talked to me every night on the phone for hours.

We cried together, we laughed together, and she felt the pain that I was going through. She dedicated her time to me for many years to get me through my grief. I will never forget her devotion to helping me through this. They say that God puts certain people in your life for a reason. I could not have asked for a better friend. When we finished talking, my daughter would take over by telling me that I was going to get through this and that she loved me. She would tell me all the time how happy she was, and that made me happy for the moment. At night is when the grief was heavy. I felt alone in my sorrow. I know she was there, but I could not see her.

One day, I was reading a circular and came across a counselor who specialized in grief. As I read about her, I was happy to know that she was also spiritual. I had decided to make an appointment with her. She was in the next town and had an office where she lived. On my first appointment, I had told her that I could hear my daughter speaking to me. I had told her about the first time I had heard my daughter speak to me at the funeral home. I was happy to know that she believed in me and made me feel comfortable to be able to speak about my daughter and what she was saying to me. I remember when my daughter was telling me that she was in atonement where you go over your life with the masters and teachers. It was to understand your path in life, and it was talked over with no judgment but love.

I would also talk about my pain and how I was trying to cope with it. Each time I left her office, I felt better. I was able to talk about my feeling and talk about Erica. When the night came, the pain let me know that it was there. I would sit for hours just crying, and Dakota would try to comfort me by putting his head on my lap. Erica would try to get my attention by flicking the lights on and off which would make me stop crying to hear her voice. There were many times when she tried to talk to me, but I could not hear her through my tears. She would hit the dog's tail while he was sleeping on his bed to wake him up. He would follow her to her picture on the wall and bark so I would know that she wanted to talk to me. She was trying to comfort me and let me know that she was alive in spirit and that she loved me and was going to help me get through this.

There were times when I was angry at Erica, and I let her know it. I had asked her how she could have done this to herself and to me. "Why would you use knowing that this could have been an outcome of your use? How could you have done this to me?" She would try to explain, but I had told her that I did not want to hear it. She would tell me that she was sorry, and I would tell her that sorry does not bring you back. I would be angry for days and block her out. She would be tapping on the glass, and I would ignore her. When the anger had passed, I would hear Erica. She had told me that many

times she had tried to quit, but she would go back because it was hard. I had told her that I did not understand why it was hard to let go of drugs. She told me that someday you will understand. I did not know what she had meant by that. I wanted to understand now. I wanted answers. I had asked her if those people had hurt her. I asked if she was the guinea pig to use the drug. I got no answers.

I went to counseling once a week. I would talk about how it was hard at work being around people, doing my job, and trying not to cry. The pain would be so bad at times that I would be sick to my stomach. I knew the pain was showing on my face, but it was hard to hide. At times people whom my daughter knew would come into the store to shop and would tell me that they heard about Erica and asked what had happened. It was hard to keep myself from crying when I would explain to them what happened. I knew it was good for me to be at work, but it was so hard to focus on my job.

Erica would speak to me at work, and it would help me get through the day because I knew she was with me. One counseling session when the counselor told me that it was my daughter's life, it was about her journey made me feel discounted to Erica. I felt that she was telling me that Erica was not a part of me, and for that reason, I no longer went to counseling. I do know now why I felt that way. I believe that I was struggling with the idea that because my daughter was no longer here, that I was no longer a mother. I was not sure if could still call myself a mother. When someone asked me if I have any children, I did not know what to say. I struggled with this for a long time.

The counselor had told me about a group for parents who had lost children, and I decided to look into it. The group met once a week at night in a church hall. Everyone made me feel welcome. We would sit in a circle, and each person had a chance to talk about their grief. I come to realize that I was feeling the same as everyone else was. It made me feel a little better knowing that I was not alone in my grief. This gave me some comfort, and I felt like a mother again. I was Erica's mother, and I always will be. I attended for a year, and it was immensely helpful with my grief, but I needed to move on.

I will always be grateful for this group, the wonderful people I met who made me feel welcome and that I was not alone with my pain.

The signs kept coming that Erica was around. She would still tap on the glass lights or make the light go on and off. She would have the dog's attention in which he would look up at the corner of the ceiling and follow her around the room. At times, I would feel like a feather touching the side of my face or on my hand. I knew she was there, and it made me happy. I knew that I was blessed to have this wonderful gift from God—to be able to know my daughter was still here and speaking to me.

I knew my daughter was a wonderful person and that she loved me and wanted to help me through this. When I visited her grave at the cemetery, she would tell me that she was not there. She knew that each time I went there, it caused much pain. It was hard to separate the fact that her body was there, but it was not where she was. I guess I still could not believe that I could hear and speak to my daughter. It kept feeling as though it was not reality, but in fact it was. I heard my daughter tell me every day that she loved me and that she was helping me through this. I started feeling guilty that she was focused on helping me. I had asked her if she was supposed to be doing something else, and I was taking her from what she was supposed to be doing. She told me that she was also working on the other side. She was working with children. I was so proud of her and happy that she was finally happy on the other side.

I knew that my daughter had much grief in her life when she was here. She had many challenges which would cause her much pain. I am truly grateful to God that my daughter is in a good place and that she is happy. Erica told me that many children die from an awful experience and carry that trauma with them to the other side. She said she works with them to help them through the trauma so they can feel the peace and love which is around them. I felt so proud of her. I knew she was good with children because I had seen her many times with her friends' children. Many times, she had babysat and had much patience and love for them. I knew that this was meant for her to do this work on the other side.

It was hard carrying around a broken heart. All my friends had children who grew up with my daughter. Many times, I would want to talk about Erica, but my friends thought it would make me sad, and so the subject was dropped. I did not want to act as though my daughter did not exist. There were times when I was invited to family functions and felt alone while I was there. Erica would then comfort me by talking to me so I would not feel alone.

The holidays were extremely hard, especially Christmas. I could not celebrate Christmas by buying gifts and exchanging them. I felt that if I could not celebrate with Erica, then I did not want to celebrate at all. I celebrated that it was about Jesus, his birth, and put the manager out, but that was all that I could do. When my daughter's birthday came around, it was as though I was in another world. I could not function at all on her birthday. I had gotten better through the years with the holidays. I still do not celebrate Christmas, but hopefully someday I will. I know Erica would like me to, but I am not there yet. I know that our loved ones want us to go on with our lives. They do not want to see us unhappy and grieving all the time. They are going on with their lives on the other side. They are happy, and they want us to be happy as well.

There were times when I would tell myself that I will see her again on the other side. It seemed like a longtime that I would be on the other side, so then I decided that I would pretend that she is still living but in another state. Then I thought that this is simply crazy to think this way. I needed to face reality and by pretending I was not. I needed to accept the fact that yes, I will see her again on the other side when it is my time. Not to pretend because that was not real. I would only make myself worst if I thought this way, and I wanted to get better and not have this pain in my heart for the rest of my life. It is funny how the mind works sometimes.

Erica had told me that the other side was like earth, but you do not feel sadness or pain. She said that it was beautiful there. The feeling of peace and love was all around and the love for humanity here on earth. I had thought what a wonderful feeling that must be to feel that way all the time. Erica knew what I was thinking and had many times given me a feeling of peace and love. It was like a wave washing over me, and I knew what she was feeling all the time. It was wonderful, but it did not last long only a moment, but I was thankful to feel what she was feeling. She would say, "Mom, this is what I feel all the time."

What a blessing to have a wonderful daughter. What a blessing to have this gift. I knew that I was to share this gift with others, to help them through their grief, and to help them understand that our loved ones who are on the other side are always with us and always there to help us. Many times, when I felt down, I would be driving in the car or outside in the yard, I would see a flash of pink in the sky. This was my sign from my daughter that she was sending me love. She knew I was feeling down or depressed because I was missing her. She wanted me to know that she was with me and that she loved me.

This would happen many times among other signs. I spoke about my daughter and my gift to many people at work and friends. Some to help with the death of a loved one and others because they wanted to hear about the other side. Many times, a loved one of a friend or coworker would speak to me from the other side and ask me to give a message. I knew that this had brought this person peace, and I was grateful to be able to do this for them. The more I spoke to people about this, the better it was for me with my grief. It felt as though this was my purpose that through the loss of my daughter, I would be able to help others with their loss. This was giving me strength and meaning in my life. I felt as though I had a purpose. Erica had told me that she had to pass on for me to fulfil my purpose here. That was hard for me to hear, but now it is my goal to fulfil my purpose.

The first two years after my daughter passed was hard. I had never felt closure in knowing why and how it happened. I never received any information from the police as to why it happened and why didn't anyone help her. It was as though she was not important enough. This made me angry and bitter, and I did not like the way I felt. Erica kept telling me, "Let it go, Mom. I am happy, and I forgive them," but I did not forgive them. How could I? My daughter was gone she will never be here with me, and I will never be able to hug her and enjoy her being here.

They were still moving on with their lives without any remorse. The pain in my heart was still there, but I was learning to live with it. I do not think that it will ever go away. In the two years, many of Erica's friends came into the store where I worked and stopped to speak to me. They would tell me of a memory they had of Erica which would make me happy. They would tell me that they missed her. Sometimes I would hear Erica laughing of the story they were telling me. I was grateful for those memories. It would get me through the day.

I started speaking more to people at work and to my friends about the afterlife. This became part of my reality that I was not going to hide it from people that I could hear my daughter and that she was helping me through this. I was happy that we were still a part of each other. Erica would tell me that we are all connected to each other and to God. We are all one and one in God. When I was growing up, I always attended church and took my first communion and confirmation, but I never really understood spirituality. I never understood the gifts of the spirit and how he is in us and knows us.

Many times during my childhood, I would dream, and the next day the dream became reality. I started to feel energy from people who were around me and sometimes their pain. I never understood why this was happening to me, and I never told anyone in fear that people would think I was crazy, so I just lived with it. I had wished that there was someone whom I could have talked to about this. Now I feel blessed and want to use my gift to help others. Through the years, I had worked at different stores and spoke to many people about my gift of hearing my daughter. Some believed and wanted to hear and learn more, and others wanted to hear more to believe.

I was not afraid to let people know about my gift because it was important to help others understand that we live and do not die if we believe in Jesus who saved us and that our loved ones are always around to help us. Some were of unfamiliar cultures and different beliefs that I shared my story with, and in turn, they shared their stories as well. We helped each other through various times in each other's lives. Some due to the loss of a loved one. This opened a new world to me, a spiritual world. The happiness that this brought to me to be able to help others with their grief and to understand how our loved ones are always around and helping us.

In the years to come, I learned my father had lung cancer which had traveled to his brain. When he went to the doctors and a biopsy was done, it was too late for treatment to save his life. He was stage 4 and deteriorating fast. The doctor suggested that he have radiation to help him think again so to get his affairs in order and to say goodbye. A friend of mine suggested that I learn Reiki to help my dad with his passing.

I learned Reiki 1 and began using it to help my dad with anxiety and pain. He had told me that it was helping him to relax which helped him with the pain. When he passed, he later told me that the Reiki helped more than you will ever know. I was grateful that I was able to help him with this. Learning Reiki opened me up more spiritually. I'd done Reiki on many people, and through Reiki, I was able to receive messages from the other side for my clients as well as helping with anxiety, depression, and pain.

This made me happy to know that I was helping someone. I felt as though I was accomplishing something in my life instead of working every day for myself and feeling grief. Doing Reiki and being able to hear loved ones from the other side was a new path, a new beginning, a new purpose in my life, and I was aware of how it made me feel. It was wonderful.

Erica was with me every day. From the time I woke up to the time I went to bed. She would tell me, "Mom, I love you, and I am here with you," which would put a smile on my face. This would get me through the days and years of my loss. There were days when I said to myself why am I getting out of bed, what do I have to live for my daughter is not here, and what is the point, then I would hear Erica telling me that she was here and that she loved me and was going to help me.

She would tell me that she was happy, and this moved me in the right direction. That was all I had ever wanted was for her to be happy. I kept reminding myself when she was here, she had many struggles which brought her unhappiness, but now she is happy, and

that brought me happiness as well and motivated me to move forward in life.

After many years had gone by, I had started having a feeling of restlessness which hung over me. It felt as though I was supposed to be doing something else but did not understand what. I had asked my daughter if she understood what was coming over me. She told me that when the time was right for me to know, I would have the answer. It was an unsettling feeling which I had felt every day for many years.

One day as I was walking my dog, Dakota, I had tripped over a piece of metal that was sticking out of the sidewalk. I put my hand out to brace myself from the fall and broke two fingers. I sat there in pain for a few minutes. My fingers that were broken were throbbing. I looked around for my dog and heard him barking. I got up and looked for him and realized he walked into a yard, up someone's stairs, and was barking at their door. He was trying to get someone to help me. He was an amazing dog. I called for him and told him that I was okay. He came, and I walked him back home holding my hand up to stop the throbbing pain.

I went to the hospital to have my fingers reset. As I was waiting in the room for the doctor to come in, I heard my daughter tell me that she was with me. I had a feeling to look up at the corner of the room, and there was Erica's face smiling at me. I could not believe what I was seeing. This was the first time in the years she had passed that I was able to see her face. She was outlined in white, and her features were white. I was so happy to see her, and I thanked her for being there with me. She told me that she did not want me to be alone, and at that moment, I felt her love inside of me. I had only seen her for a few seconds, but I was so grateful to have those seconds and to feel her love for me. I have been truly blessed.

Many times, we talked, and at one time, I had asked for her forgiveness. When she was here with me, there were times when we would argue and say hurtful words to each other. I was not the greatest with patience and understanding. It was an opportunity to let her know that I was sorry for the way I had treated her and that I love her. Even though you may not be able to see or speak to your loved ones, they are there, and they can hear you when you speak to them. My mother at one time was speaking to my father who is on the other side. She could not see or hear him, but she knew that he was around her. I had taken her to the bank the next day and waited in the car for her.

My father started speaking to me and told me to tell my mother that he forgives her and that he loves her. When my mother came back to the car, I had told her what my father had said to tell her. She had told me that she was telling him the night before that she was sorry for some of the things she had done and said to him when he was here. She told me she was happy that he had heard her.

My daughter kept telling me that we are connected with God's light to each other even with our loved ones on the other side. I now understand what she was telling me that we are one with our Creator. Through our Creator, we are all connected to our loved ones who have passed and with everyone on earth. I had spoken to many people about this, friends and people I had worked with. Especially if someone lost a loved one, I told them that they could speak to them and that their loved one would hear them. This would comfort them to help them through their grief. This was important to share with them whether they believed or not. This is my purpose to share with others what I have learned from my daughter. This made me want to learn more about spirituality and learn the next level of Reiki. I wanted to keep learning. I was not sure of what was next in my life, but I knew eventually I was going to find out. Maybe this was the restlessness that I was feeling.

One day, when I arrived at work at 7:00 a.m., I noticed a red piece of paper on the floor. I had this strong feeling inside me to pick it up but told myself that the cleaner was here with me and would take care of it. As I stood in front of this red paper, the feeling was stronger, so I then picked it up. I noticed that it was more than a piece of paper. It looked like a small book, and when I turned it over the cover read, "The Littlest Bible." It was the size of a matchbook and had stories of the Bible. I placed it in my purse until I had a chance to look it over. That day at work, I had received a phone call

from my manager who had informed me that after my vacation, I will be reporting to another store to work.

My vacation was the following week, and she was telling me that this was going to be my last week working in this store. I was not happy with this news. I have been working in the town in which I live, and the other location was an hour away. Throughout the years, I had worked at other locations for this company, and some were an hour away. I felt at this time that I was not going to travel anymore and wanted to stay at the location that I was working in. I had also gone home at lunchtime to check on my mother. She had trouble walking and was showing signs of dementia. I had told this to the district manager and told him that I was also having problems with my vehicle. He told me that he would get back to me the following day with his decision. I knew in my heart that I was going to have to go to this location, so I had made up my mind that I was going to terminate my employment with the company.

With that in mind, I decided to start cleaning out my desk. Over my desk, I had a basket in which I would put important papers in, so I decided to start going through the paperwork. In front of me was another Bible that was under the paperwork. I could not believe what I was looking at. I had never seen this Bible before. I asked all my coworkers if it belonged to anyone or if they know who had put it there. No one had seen it before, but someone had said it was a military Bible. I opened the Bible, and someone had written inside the cover Matthew and the verse number.

I looked up the verse, and I could not believe what I had seen. The verse read, "Let yes be yes and no be no and anything in between was the work of the devil." I was amazed at what I was seeing. This was a sign for me to move on. This was the restlessness that I was feeling for a long time. The following day, I received the phone call that I was to take the position at the other location, or he was taking my resignation. I resigned.

As soon as I hung up the phone, a feeling of peace had come over me in which I had never felt before. The feeling of restlessness was gone, and it was replaced with this wonderful feeling of peace. I was not afraid of what my future was going to be. I was at peace, and I knew that Jesus was with me, holding me up and moving me forward. I felt as though I was walking on air as I finished my last shift of work. I had told the employees that I was leaving, and many were upset. I told them that it was time for me to move on from here and would stay in touch with them. I explained that I knew I was moving on my path because the restlessness was gone and replaced with peace. They were happy for me, and I was grateful for that.

I had worked over thirty years in retail management, and now I was on a new journey in my life. I was not sure what was next, but I knew that Jesus was guiding me. A few weeks had passed, and I was still feeling peace. I was not afraid of what the future would bring. I trusted Jesus to show me what I needed to do. I had applied for unemployment and had to appeal because I was denied. I eventually was able to collect for six months. In that time, a friend of mine had mention to me about going back to school to be a substance abuse counselor. I knew that there was an epidemic of people dying from drug abuse, and I thought how wonderful it would be to help people achieve getting off drugs. I would do this in honor of my daughter, Erica. I looked into where I could study and found out that it was offered in the next town from where I lived. I applied and started in the following weeks.

A new beginning at life. I had wanted for a long time to get out of retail, and now it has come true. I had thought of ways to start a new career but never could see it happening because of my schedule at work. It made the idea impossible. Now my wish was coming true. If anyone would have told me that I was going to be a substance abuse counselor, I would told them they were crazy. Now I was going to learn about addiction and help people with their addiction. I was excited but also sad because I had wished I could have helped my daughter with her addiction. Erica would tell me not to be sad that she was proud of me that I wanted to help others. Still, it would have been wonderful to have been able to help my daughter.

I was nervous about going back to school and learning something different. I was a lot older and was unsure about being able to process the studying and tests that was involved. I knew that this was the right course for me to take, so I talked myself out of the fear.

There was a lot to learn about addiction and what the drug does to your mind and body. I kept thinking about what my daughter had gone through and learned that it was extremely hard to fight the addiction. It brought up guilt of how I treated my daughter and that made the course difficult.

There were times when I wanted to cry because of the way I had treated my daughter. To learn how difficult it is to stop using and my ignorance of thinking that if you really want to you can, I know now that this is not so. I cried many nights and asked for her forgiveness. I felt ashamed of what I had said and done to her. I had wished I had taken the time to be more supportive toward her. I was no support for her when she needed me. I did not know that the drug takes over a part of your mind, changes your personality, and numbs your feelings.

When a person is in addiction, all they can think about is when they can use again. They do not eat or sleep, and they put themselves in dire situations to obtain money for the drug. Many times, I would see Erica skinny, I knew she was not eating. It was devastating as a parent to see your child do this to themselves. If you do not understand addiction, it makes it even worse to see them that way. You feel disgusted that they would put themselves through a life like this. When the drug starts wearing off, they go into withdrawals which are painful on the body. It causes pain so they would rather use again instead of going through the pain. The withdrawal symptoms are like flu-like symptoms which causes vomiting, pain in the stomach, pain in your legs and all over your body, headaches, and sometimes a fever. This stage is called the post-acute stage of addiction.

When you make it through the post-acute stage, then you go into the acute stage of addiction. This is the mind stage in which you start feeling your feelings. They are not the good feelings of happiness. They are the feeling of depression, anxiety, and shame. The thoughts come back to what you did while using and the people who you hurt and how you hurt yourself. The receptors in the brain that make you feel are now regenerating to heal itself. The drug caused the receptors to stop and not regenerate which made the person who was using numb to their feelings. You do not care about yourself or anyone else when using.

This acute stage goes on for years that is why many people relapse repeatedly. It is like a never-ending battle when you are trying to stay away from the drug. That is why they need support from their family and friends. They need counseling and encouragement to go on with their lives because it is a daily fight. I know I had to take this journey to understand and to help other parents help their child who is in addiction. I know the path that my daughter took enabled me to be on my path of what I am doing now. It took a year and a half to finish classes, and I had started looking for work in this field.

Erica encouraged me every day, and I would talk to her about things that had applied to her about her addiction. I had learned that she tried many times to put herself in treatment. They had helped for a while, but she ended up relapsing again. Addiction is a hard, drawn-out battle, and if you are not in a good place in your mind or your environment when trying to stay clean, you relapse. What I mean by that is you need your basic needs met like shelter, food, and clothing. You also need support from family and friends, and you definitely need your hopes and dreams. You need a goal for your life and to work toward that goal. You need to set a plan, a step-by-step plan, of how you are going to achieve that goal. You need a purpose in your life. You need a reason to want to stay clean.

I had found a position in the city in which I lived. It was not for substance abuse counselor but for recovery specialist. I had taken this position because I felt that I would better understand hands on about helping others in addiction as well as being close to home. I was told that when an opening came up for counselor, I could apply. The position was part-time, but I needed full-time employment. The manager had told me that if I am interested in working all departments and working for two managers, they could work something out where I would have full time, and so I was hired. I was told that it was the first time that they ever had someone work for both managers to acquire full time.

I worked in all the departments which was great for learning everything. I took care of the patients when they first came in and

was going through withdrawal. Most of the time when they first came in, they would sleep a lot. It was hard to see them going through the withdrawals. Some had it harder than others, and it depended on what they were using and how long they had been using. I learned how to take their pulse and their blood pressure and would check on them in their room to make sure they were doing okay. I would take them to their cigarette breaks and take them down to the cafeteria for dinner if they were not too sick. I would do groups with them and try to get them involved with the group. When they started feeling a little better, it was easier to speak with them. I also worked in dual diagnosis which is when they have a mental health issue as well as addiction.

Then the other half of the week, I would work in the step-down units which the ladies and the men were on separate units. This was the acute stage where they start getting feelings back which are depression, shame, anxiety, and other mental health issues. This is when you would see them struggling with their emotions. Every day was a battle for them. It was sometimes hard because you would be working with all different personalities who were going through all different emotions. This is the stage in which counseling, groups, and understanding was important. This was the department where you would help them go into more treatment after they left this facility.

Halfway houses are where they would live and work on their treatment or they would go home to loved ones and go to treatment during the day. They needed to be convinced that there were programs out there that could help them—a place where they could get back on their feet, a roof over their head, a job, and a sense of belonging, being part of society. We would talk to them about going to group meeting or AA meetings.

Sometimes it was hard to convince them into going to further treatment because they thought that they had it beat because they were there. Some did not want to hear that it takes time to keep themselves from relapsing especially when they went back to the same neighborhood where they used. Those were triggers, and it was only a matter of time when you would see them back again. I was glad that they were trying again and that they did not overdose. It was sad to hear of someone who left, and weeks or months later, you had heard that they had overdosed. It used to break my heart.

During groups I would sometimes tell them about Erica, and most were grateful that I was helping them after losing my daughter. I sometimes gave them a parent's point of view about their addiction, which helped them understand why their parents did not know what to do to help them, even if they were told that they had to leave the home to try to have them understand that they were not just hurting themselves but their families as well. Some could understand, and others could not because of the way their childhood was when they were growing up. Sometimes it was hard to believe what so many went through in their life and the pain that it caused them. Many would use drugs to numb the pain of the life that they had. It was so heartbreaking to hear how they managed this far in life.

One day when I was working on the post-acute unit, one of the counselors had asked if I had a picture of my daughter Erica. I had told them about my daughter and told some that I was able to communicate with her. I showed her a picture of Erica which I carried around in my purse. When she looked at the picture, her reply was, "Oh my god." I had asked her what was wrong, and she said, "You are not going to believe this." She walked over to the nurse's Roladex and flipped it to the back, and there was my daughter's obituary.

Someone had laminated it and put it in the back of the Roladex. I could not believe what I was seeing. I asked if she knew who had put her obituary there, and she did not know but knew that it was there since she had passed. I had asked everyone who worked there if they knew who had put it there, and they had not. I had also learned that my daughter had gone there for treatment. I never knew. She never told me that she had gone there. It hurt me inside to know that the place where I was working is where my daughter came for help. The rooms that I worked in was where she was at one time, and I did not know until now. I knew that this was another sign that I was on my right path, but it caused a lot of pain inside.

I had worked in this position for about a year and a half in which I started feeling restless again. A position had opened for substance abuse counselor, and I applied. I was offered the position where I

would work in the step-down unit which was the acute units. I was working with them one-on-one and doing groups. I found counseling rewarding. I was contributing to society by helping people work through their addiction. They would tell me why they started using. Some were because of the lifestyle their parents gave them or because a doctor started them on pain killers. I would hear how they could not take it anymore the way they were living. Some had lost their children and was trying to get them back. Others wanted their parents back in their lives.

There were so many reasons, but what it came down to was they wanted themselves back to who they were before their addiction. I remember all the times my daughter would say that she wanted her life back. I wished that she had gotten herself back, for she would be here with me now. I know that she is happy and safe, and I am grateful to know that. This did give me some comfort. She would tell me many times that she was proud of me doing this work to help others. She told me that she was also doing work in addiction on the other side.

When a person would overdose, they would wake up on the other side and not know what had happened to them. Some could not accept that they had passed and were not going back. My daughter would help them through it to accept what had happened. I am so proud of her and happy to know that we are both doing the same work, helping others with their addiction. This made me feel even more connected to her.

There were days when it was tuff in this field. Sometimes there would be someone who was ungrateful that you were helping them. They would not want to talk when in counseling, and in group, they would disrupt the class. I knew that it was hard for them, so I tried not to take it personal and instead try to show them understanding and respect. The stigma about addiction is terrible, and it causes low self-esteem.

In groups, sometimes I would speak about my daughter's journey in addiction. I spoke from my heart, and many times, I had cried during class which many showed their compassion. Many realized that it was hard for me to talk about my daughter and work in this field. They understood that I was compassionate about helping them. They would then show respect toward me and the class. I was getting through to some people and others not so much. I am sure that the feelings that were flooding them had a lot to do with the way they were acting.

I had asked the manager if I could use Reiki on them to help them with anxiety and depression, and I was told that I could. The following day after doing Reiki on some, they would tell me that they had lots of energy and felt happy. Reiki balances the energy centers that we have in our body. They are called chakras, and they have functions throughout our body. When they are in alignment, you feel balanced. Reiki clears blockages from anxiety, depression, pain, and trauma. Reiki clears negative energy which helps clear your mind and soul and relaxes your body. Soon, I had a line that was waiting on Reiki which I was happy to do for them.

There were times when I wanted to crawl in a corner and shut the world out. Those were the times when my daughter would be around me more. She would tell me she was happy, that she missed me, and what she has been doing on the other side. She would give me a pep talk about how this was my purpose to help others and to stay strong. She would do this for me all the time when it was hard to deal with the pain of losing her. I still could not get through the idea that I was never going to see her again in my lifetime.

There were times when I would feel love come over me, and I knew my daughter was showing me the love that she was feeling. I knew that she loved me and that she knew that I loved her. We always get help from our loved ones on the other side. We get busy with our lives, and we do not see the signs that they are trying to communicate with us to help us. We need to give time for prayer and listening. I am profoundly grateful for my gift of hearing my daughter and to know that she is always around encouraging and helping me.

Another job had crossed my path that was out of town. It did pay more money which I needed. I applied and was offered the job which I accepted. The position was still in substance abuse, but it was more groups and now helping them with aftercare. I was nervous about working there because it was at a prison. It was men sectioned

from the court and placed in a prison environment that was run by the department of corrections. There was really no one-on-one counseling. The men were receiving their counseling through groups which were at least four or more a day. It did not take long for me to settle into the way things were done.

All the counselors worked together in one room and made me feel welcome. All the different personalities were in one room, and it worked. We all helped each other. Most of the work was finding them aftercare. Some went to halfway houses, some went to sober houses, some went to shelters, and some went home to families. It was our job to make sure that they were doing aftercare for their recovery. It was an exhausting job, but it was rewarding. Not all days were good. Most patients of course did not like the idea that they were there and could not leave. They especially did not like the idea of being in a prison and treated like a prisoner.

You would have some patients try to take over the class about being there, and I would have to stop the problem before it got out of hand. This would be the time when I would hear Erica help me by saying do not take it personal—not to focus on my feelings but what they were going through. That would make me feel better. There were times when I would let them vent but only to a certain extent because the situation could get out of hand. I never had a problem with that because I knew when to stop it, and I did not want any of the patients to get into trouble.

In this position, I learned to have more patience and empathy than I ever had before. I remember a day when I was getting ready to do a class with the older population. As I was looking out at them to take attendance, I felt their brokenness and vulnerability. I also felt love for them. As I started speaking to them, a wave of knowledge took over me. It was as though someone was speaking through me. I had never experienced that before. It was amazing. This had happened several times after, and I welcomed it. It was always done with the feeling of love. It was so incredible. I was so blessed to be able to experience these words of knowledge flowing through me to help these men. The men felt the love through the words because they commented about the peace they felt and called me Debra Love. I knew that I was getting help to help these men.

I enjoyed going to work every day because I was making a difference with these men. I was getting encouragement from my daughter every day, telling me that she was proud of me and that she was helping me. I also knew that I was getting help with knowledge about addiction from the other side to help these men. It was hard to see them broken down physically and mentally, but we knew how to show them encouragement and empathy to help them move forward in their recovery.

Most would go on to further treatment and be successful at staying clean. Others we would hear that they had given in to their addiction. Some would come back, and we would tell them that it was okay that it does happen and that we were happy they were okay. Some would not make it back. We would hear that they had lost their battle with addiction. This would break our hearts. It was hard to hear this. My daughter would tell me that she was helping them on the other side, and I knew that she was giving them the love and attention that they needed. I know that it may be hard to think this way, but it was easy for me because I could hear my daughter and knew that it was so.

Some of the men after leaving the facility would call the counselor who had helped them and would talk about their progress. This made it all worthwhile to know that they were accomplishing staying clean, was working a job, and was feeling better about themselves. They had a goal and was working toward it. Some would say that their children had forgiven them and was back in their lives. I was so happy to her about their accomplishments. It made us feel that the job was worth doing. Sometimes I would receive a letter or a card thanking me for helping them. Sometimes it would just take my breath away.

As I worked in this position for two years, it became easy to look past the mistakes that they had made in their lives. They are people like you and I who got caught up in addiction. Some people would say that they choose to use, but that is not true. They did not wake up one day and say that they wanted to be an addict. It has to

do with the mental pain that they have inside them. The pain that could be from loss or trauma that they had in their lives. It could have been from a prescription that they got from the doctor for pain. They did not seek help, and when they found something in a drug to numb the pain, they thought that it feels better than what they were feeling before the drug. Some did not realize that they have mental health problems, so they did not seek treatment.

We need to look past the mistakes and see the good in them. Not to judge them like society does on the stigma of addiction but to help them realize that no one is better than anyone else and we all make mistakes. I felt this and believed in it—to help them see past their weakness that they have strength to fight this and that they are not defined by their addiction and that they are like everyone else and deserving of love. I wanted them to believe this so it would give them strength and see themselves differently instead of punishing themselves. Most of them felt shame because of the stigma of addiction. That is why they needed to understand that they are worthy of being clean and not a prisoner of their addiction.

At the end of the two years, COVID-19 came into our lives. Everything started shutting down, and it stopped the men from coming into treatment. We could no longer send them to further treatment because everyone was shutting down even the shelters. All we could do at this time was to release them when their time was up and hope and pray that they stay clean. Many were afraid of going out there on their own because of the fear of relapse and that there would be no help for them. I knew that this was not a good thing and that many would not make it, but there was no choice to make.

I felt terrible that we could not place these men and we were sending them out into the world with no help in place. We all felt this. At this time, I had let a patient use the phone in the office which was a no on the property of the department of corrections. They had found out that I had done this and walked me off the property. I could no longer work there. This was my time to move on to my next journey. I no longer felt useful there, so I was happy to leave.

This was the time when everything was shutting down, and we had to stay in our homes because of COVID-19. I had saved some money, so I had lived off the savings until I could collect. In this time, I had thought about what my next step should be. Would I stay in substance abuse or move on to something else. I prayed and asked for guidance, and my prayers were answered. It was to write a book about how my daughter helped me from the other side. This is to help others understand how our loved ones are always with us and helping us and how we come here with a purpose.

So now I am writing this book with the intention of it helping many people. May it be that someone in the family is fighting addiction, and you are a parent with the need to understand, or it be that you have lost someone and are grieving this person. Either way, I hope this book brings comfort and peace. My journey has not stopped here. I felt the need to learn about grief more and took a course online to have a better understanding. Then my next intention is to learn more about spirituality—our connection with God through our soul.

A course was offered for the first time about spirituality, and I knew that it was something I should do. I felt myself being drawn to learn. It was a ten-month course which you end up having a bachelor's in divinity and you become an interfaith minister. I was home and not working, so it was a perfect opportunity to learn. I am still learning through different courses that I have been taking. I have been praying to learn what my next journey is, and I hear that this book is going to take me places. It is indeed a journey that I had never thought possible, but nothing is impossible with God.

# Author's Note

As I sit back and contemplate all the years that have gone by without my daughter, I am amazed at how my life has changed drastically for the better. I know that it sounds strange to think that, but the experience of the loss of my daughter has changed my life. It has brought me to years of learning to the excitement of writing this book—a book in which I hope will help many people to find comfort in their grief and to understand that God is always with us and wanting to help as well as our loved ones who has returned home.

I have never thought my life would have gone in the direction that it did. I feel blessed to feel God's love and guidance. A path of spiritual awareness, wonderment, and knowledge is given to me as gifts to help others is such a wonderful experience. It has taught me to be grateful for life and for what I have in my life and to be able to use my experience of loss to help others.

With this book, I hope to let people know that God has put us here for a reason. He took my pain and made it into something real for me to share with others. Through all this, I have learned Reiki and became a Reiki master through the Sisters of Solace Holistic Healing

Center in Westport, Massachusetts. I have used Reiki through the years and continue to do so.

A ministry program had crossed my path which I felt a strong need to attend. I have wanted to learn more about spirituality for a long time, and this was the first time this program was offered at The Soul Purpose in Swansea, Massachusetts. I am now an inter-faith minister at the Birch Tree Sanctuary, at the Soul Purpose, and a member of the Universal Brotherhood Movement Inc. I have helped at the Soul Purpose doing spiritual cleansing with prayer and Reiki.

As I am writing this, I am so amazed that my life has gone in this direction. I feel truly blessed every day for where God has taken me, and I look forward to the future for more happiness to come.

This book has brought me peace, and I truly hope whoever reads this book will find peace as well.

God bless!

Debra Ann Maciel